The CHRISTMAS ROCKET

THE
CHRISTMAS
ROCKET

ANNE MOLLOY
with drawings by
ARTUR MAROKVIA

HASTINGS HOUSE, PUBLISHERS, NEW YORK

Copyright © 1958, by Hastings House, Publishers, Inc.
Copyright © 1957, by Anne Molloy. Originally published as
THE FOUR LEGS OF GIAN CARLO in *The Horn Book,* December 1957

Library of Congress Catalog Card Number: 58-8274

Printed in the United States of America

They took turns choosing.

There were three of them in the old pottery workshop, Dino, his father, and his grandfather. The two men were potters and someday Dino would be a potter, too. Once upon a time both the men had looked as Dino did now. Like him, they had been brown-eyed and dark-haired, thin and wiry. Now the grandfather was as shriveled as an old pea with a knitted cap upon his bald head. Papa's back was stooped from work.

Today they were busy choosing the finest dishes from among the piles on the earthen floor. First Dino chose one, and then Papa. Sometimes the old grandfather left the wheel where he was shaping pots and picked one out, too.

Their choices were very important. Tomorrow was the day before Christmas. Dino and Papa were to carry their pots and plates, their cups and pitchers down the mountainside to sell them in the town. They must pick out dishes so beautiful that they would surely sell. And they would, Dino was sure. Papa was the finest pottery painter in all of Italy. Dino had heard that many times in his little village.

The boy felt very important as he helped. This would be his first trip with Papa. The old grandfather had always gone before but now his legs were good only for turning the potter's wheel. They could no longer carry him so far down the mountain and back again.

Until last year their old donkey, Maria-Luisa, had carried their wares in great baskets hung on her sleek sides. But she had died and there had been no money to buy another donkey. After that Papa and the old grandfather had to carry the pottery in baskets on their own backs. Tomorrow Dino would take the grandfather's place.

Dino picked up a bowl. He turned it slowly between his hands
in the same direction as the red and blue painted fish were swim-
ming around its sides. "This bowl," he said, "this bowl will surely
sell tomorrow. You *are* a good artist, Papa. And when we sell it,
then surely we can buy some meat for our Christmas dinner.
We've always had meat for dinner on Christmas."

"Don't depend on it this year," Papa said. "Let me see. This
pitcher now, we'll take this. It is a good stout one and it pours
well.

And if I do say so, I painted the fruit on it better than usual. Yet, we ought to charge a good price for it. We might even get a pair of shoes for you, Dino. Mama has been feeling sad all day. 'Here is our son Dino,' she keeps saying, 'He is a great boy, almost ten, and chosen to carry a candle in our church procession on Christmas Eve. He will be the only one in it without shoes. All the others, they will make a good sound with their leather shoes and Dino won't even make the horrid clump of those cheap wooden zoccoli'."

"Ho, it will be quite dark near my feet," said Dino. "I will hold my candle high. No one will see that *my* feet are the silent ones."

He was searching for the platter that was his next choice. It was a big one, large enough for Papa's painting of the family working at their grape harvest. They were all there on the platter, even poor old Maria-Luisa, the donkey.

"Here, put this one in," he said when he found it. "I like it although you did paint me on it with too long a nose. Somebody rich could buy this platter and fill it with food for the Christmas Birthday. Perhaps if they did buy it I could get one rocket to shoot off outside the church at midnight on Christmas Eve. My friend Mario has already bought three rockets."

He laid down the platter on the straw beside the other chosen dishes.

"Perhaps," said Papa.

"Rockets," said the grandfather, exploding like one." Rockets! They go up fast with a *fizz* and then what do you have left? A stick, if you can find it. That is all."

They kept on choosing until they had enough pottery to fill Papa's big basket and the small one that Dino would carry. By the time both were carefully packed it was very late. Dino had never stayed up so late before except on Christmas Eve.

On the way home to bed, they stopped outside the workshop door. They looked down toward the town where they would go tomorrow. The sky was full of stars that twinkled fast because the wind blew cold. Far down the mountainside they could see the stars of the sea, the fishermen's lights, bobbing on the water. The men must be out bringing in a good catch for Christmas Eve.

Dino let out a great sigh. "If only we could sell all our pottery tomorrow, every bit! Then we could buy Enrico's young donkey to carry our bowls and platters. Enrico says he will soon sell him to someone else. He needs the money. He cannot wait much longer for ours. I have named the young donkey already. He is Gian-Carlo. Do you like that name?"

"Yes," said Papa, "Gian-Carlo is a good name. And we do need a donkey to take poor old Maria-Luisa's place."

"When she carried our pots, *everyone* bought them," Dino reminded him. "She was such a sweet donkey! Remember how fine she looked with red tassels on her bridle? People came just to look at her. And they stayed to buy. Her baskets were almost as good as a shop. People could see all our wares spread out. When Maria-Luisa came back up the mountain at night, her baskets were empty. Empty except for the straw in them."

"Ah, yes," sighed Papa, remembering. "Her baskets would be light and my pockets heavy with money in those days. It's as if our luck flew out the window when the poor donkey died. But unless we go to bed now, we shall sell no pots at all tomorrow. And don't forget, Dino, that together you and I have as many legs as any donkey."

It was still dark the next morning when father and son went winding their way down the mountain with their heavy baskets.

They passed their old village church that was no longer used.
It was kept locked but Old Agata next door to it had the key.
She was caretaker and let visitors in to see the famous old painted
walls. She was like a dragon with a sharp tongue and a heavy
hand. In spite of this, Dino went into the church whenever he
saw the door unlocked. For he loved the paintings on the wall.
He was safe from Old Agata while the tourists were there. She
was eager for the money that they put into her open palm and
her tongue dripped only honey when they could hear.

But this morning Dino and Papa passed her house so early
that the old woman had not yet lighted her oil lamp.

Farther down and around a curve they came to the little donkey, Gian-Carlo, drowsing under an olive tree. Dino thought how happy they would be if they owned him. Like Maria-Luisa, their old donkey, he had soft, mouse-gray fur and sad, sweet eyes with long lashes. He had dainty little feet so that he minced along like a lady in high heels even when he had a heavy load on his back.

Usually Dino stopped to rub the donkey's furry back for a bit and to have a talk. Today, with pots to be sold he couldn't tarry but he did call out, "Good morning, Gian-Carlo." Then he said to Papa, "Won't it be fine when we have enough money to buy all four of Gian-Carlo's legs at once?"

Several times Dino's family had saved enough to buy two of Gian-Carlo's legs and once they had enough for three legs. Then each time they had needed money for other things and had spent it. They had had to buy oil for cooking, or cheese. Cold winds brought back the grandfather's cough and Papa had to buy medicine for him. Each time that the money had been spent, Dino was afraid that someone else would buy all four legs of Gian-Carlo before they ever could.

"Rest well, old Sleepyhead," Dino called to the donkey as they
went around the next bend.

Down, down, through farmyards and olive orchards, down long flights of steps they wound. When they reached the narrow stone-paved streets of the town where cars honked and motor-scooters hooted, Dino's heart leaped with excitement.

By this time they knew that the sun would not shine that day. The sea was an angry green. It snarled in white foam along the rocky headlands. It burst in upon the fishermen's beach. And before Papa and Dino sat down to their bread at midday, they knew that they would not sell many pots that day. Although tomorrow was Christ's Birthday and Papa was the finest painter in all Italy, no one would buy their wares. No one.

They knocked at the kitchen doors of rich houses. Each one was open by an angry cook or housemaid.

"Be off, be off," she would say, raising her arms toward the sky. "Who here has time to look at pots? Tonight we sit fourteen at table. Tomorrow on the Birthday, twenty. There's no time for all that must be done. This is no day to look at pots, or to sell them."

When Papa called out his wares in the narrow streets where
the poor folk lived, it was just as bad.

They passed a woman carrying a jug to the well for water.

"Your water jug has a broken nose," said Papa. "Buy a new one, all fresh and beautiful."

"Broken or not, I have no money for another. I have spent it all for figs and oil and meat for the Birthday," she answered.

Farther along, a woman leaned from a window. She was hanging clothes on a line overhead. She crowded them so close that their tops made scallops across the narrow alley. Her mouth was full of clothespins.

"A new pot for the Birthday, a new plate for the Feast," Papa called out to her.

The woman's ears might have been as full of clothespins as her mouth. She took no notice of him.

And so it went. At the café there was not a soul drinking coffee at the tables outside.

"Not one tourist even," cried Papa. "It is too cold and windy, or like everyone else they are too busy. Usually I can sell them something small to take home with them, like candlesticks or an ash tray.

Well, there's no use in your staying longer, Dino. I promised Mama I would send you home after our lunch. Go along home and take care of the pots. Someday we may sell them."

Dino nodded. Sadly he set out for home with his basket just as heavy as when he started out.

He quickened his steps as he passed the restaurant where his friend Mario worked. He hoped Mario would not see him, but he did. He came outside in his father's white waiter's jacket with the cuffs turned back. He patted one pocket.

"Oh, there you are, Dino," he called. "I thought you would be here earlier. See, money enough in this pocket to buy two more rockets. Let's go now to the barbershop to buy them."

"No," answered Dino, "I am going home. What are rockets? They go off *fizz,* and what do you have left? A stick, if you can find it. Good-by."

He ran up the street as fast as he could with the heavy basket on his back. He knew without turning his head that Mario's mouth would be hanging open. Dino had promised to go with him this afternoon to choose some rockets. But Mario couldn't understand what it was to have no money. His fat legs were laced into leather boots, his fat stomach was full of good soup. His father was a waiter who had a motor scooter just for pleasure.

Dino ran on and turned the first corner he came to fast. The high walls on both sides of the narrow street would hide him from Mario's sight. At the same time someone else turned the corner even faster. With a rush and a roar a motor scooter came toward him. It knocked Dino sprawling and sent his basket crashing onto the stone pavement.

The boy jumped to his feet but the motor scooter driver paused for only a moment. He wobbled his front wheeel back and forth and raced his engine while he shouted, "Stupid boy, why don't you watch where you're going? You might have killed me!" and roared off.

Dino turned to his basket and the broken pottery lying near it. The tears had been wanting and wanting to fall poured out now. Papa's fine pitcher painted with fruit had lost its handle and broken its nose. The bowl with the red and blue fish lay in two pieces. The platter, the fine platter on which Papa had painted them all, even Maria-Luisa, was smashed to bits. Dino could scarcely see through his tears to gather up the pieces.

Sadder than ever he jogged on toward home. "Take care," Papa had warned him, and see what he had done! Because he had been heedless and thinking about rockets, he had smashed their best pottery. And on his very first trip to town as Papa's helper!

He was climbing one of the long flights of steps up the mountainside when he saw old Agata coming. There was no time for him to turn off and escape her but he made himself as thin as possible to let her pass. Old Agata carried a flat leather bag and was panting in her haste. She had no thought for Dino today. "I must go down to the shops I need food for the Birthday," she cried "Surely no one will come now to see the paintings in the old church. It is getting late. The weather is too bad for tourists."

But she was wrong. When Dino came out onto the paved square before the church, there was a stranger. He was tall and wore an overcoat like a city man or tourist. He stood under the orange trees and looked down over the town and the green sea. He was wiping his forehead and breathing hard from the long climb.

Dino stopped and put down his basket.

"Did you wish to see the old church?" he asked.

"Yes," the stranger answered "I have come from far to the North and this is my only chance to see the paintings about which I have heard so much. But the church where they are is locked."

"Too bad," said Dino. "Old Agata who keeps the key has gone to town."

He was sorry that the man had climbed so far for nothing. Then, because he was proud that the paintings in their village church were so famous and because he knew as much about them as Old Agata did, he said, "I will show the paintings to you. I know all about them. I will get the church key."

Old Agata's house stood next to the church. Outside her back door were strings of dried green peppers and garlic bulbs. Under one of these strings the great key, almost as long as Dino's forearm, was hanging. He was sure of that. A dozen times at least he had seen the old woman reach for it there before she opened the church for visitors.

Dino knew by heart, too, every word that she always said about the paintings. She only recited words. When Papa told Dino about the paintings, he said what he knew and felt about them. If only Dino would really dare to open the church door, he would tell the stranger about all that Papa had taught him to admire in the pictures.

But, if Old Agata should turn back without going to town after all, she would find him inside. She would lash him with her tongue and beat him with a stick. She might even bring the policeman from town and say, "Lock up this boy, this thief. He stole my key. He planned, no doubt, to steal money from the tourists he let into the church, the little thief!"

The thought made Dino's mouth turn dry with fear and his heart thump. But he went to look for the key.

At last he found it under the bottom string of peppers. He fitted it into the great lock and the church door swung open.

At first Dino did feel like a thief, as if he were entering where he had no right to go, but after he stood on a rush-bottomed chair and turned the electric switch, his courage came back. The three bare bulbs at the end of long black cords hanging from the ceiling flashed on. The paintings on the wall stood out clearly. The visitor gasped in surprise and pleasure.

Dino told him everything that he knew about these paintings that marched around the walls. When they were first painted a very long time ago, they had been put upon the white wall to tell stories to the ordinary people who had no books and could not read. In those days only scholars could read books but anyone could read the paintings. Then, so Papa said, there had been many more colors but they had faded. Now only this warm orange and the soft rusty brown were left.

When Dino got to the three painted Wise Men hurrying to Bethlehem at the bidding of the painted Star, he talked faster and faster. Tomorrow was that same Birthday. It was very exciting.

Dino finished what he had to say and clicked out the lights as the stranger turned to go. When they had gone outside, Dino locked the heavy door. Suddenly he remembered Old Agata—she had not come after all! How lucky! He felt good as he hung the key in its place under the green pepper strings.

The stranger waited beneath the orange trees where Dino had first seen him. "Tell me," he asked, "how do you know so much about these paintings?"

"That is easy to answer." Dino grinned at him. "It is because I love them and always come in when the church is open to see them. And then Papa, who is the best painter in Italy, has told me about them."

"Does he paint pictures like them?" asked the stranger.

"Oh, no. He paints on plates and jugs and cups. Just see!"

Dino knelt on the paving stones by his basket. He took out the broken bowl with the pink and blue fish on its sides and held the two parts together. "Isn't it beautiful?" he asked.

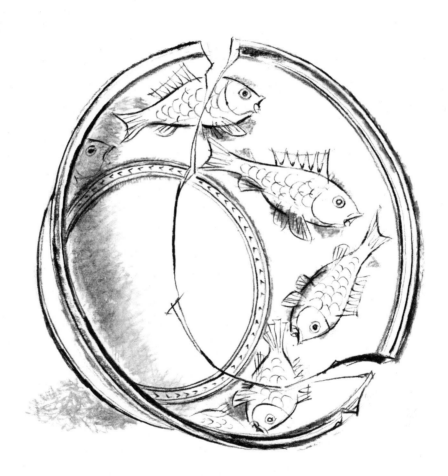

He laid the platter pieces on the stone pavement. He fitted them together carefully, like the parts of a puzzle. "This is Papa here and this is Mama and this is me and the crack where it got broken goes right through my nose. This is the grandfather and this is poor old Maria-Luisa, the donkey who died. Her baskets are full of our very own grapes. Papa paints the same things that his father and all the grandfathers before him painted on their pots. And then, too, he paints what he himself sees around him every day. Just look. Isn't this platter beautiful?"

"It is beautiful," said the stranger, "but how did it get broken?"

Dino told him how no one had bought their wares today, no one. And how on the way home a man on a motor scooter had knocked him down and broken his dishes. Sadly he began to pick up the pieces once more.

"You have been very kind to show me the old church," said the stranger. "My trip up the mountainside would have been wasted but for you. I should like to make you a present for the Birthday. What would you choose?"

Dino sat back on his heels. He thought aloud with his face turned up. "What shall I choose?" he asked himself. "If I choose a rocket, it will go off *fizz* and I will have nothing left but the stick, if I can find it, as the grandfather says. If I choose meat for our pot, that will soon be eaten and gone. If I take shoes for my feet, that will make Mama happy but the soles will wear through on the bottom. What *shall* I choose? I never have had to before. Gian-Carlo, the little donkey, is what we need the most of all, but that is too much to ask for."

He took a deep breath and said to the stranger, "I will choose one leg of Gian-Carlo. Perhaps this time we can keep the money for it until we have enough to buy the other three legs." All the time he spoke he saw in his mind beautiful rockets shooting across the sky. More than ever he wanted a rocket.

"One leg of Gian-Carlo?" asked the stranger, puzzled. "Who is he?"

Dino laughed. "Of course, you don't know." Then he told the man about the good days when Maria-Luisa had carried their wares to town. He told how everyone bought them because they looked so fine spread on the donkey's wide baskets. He told him about Gian-Carlo, the new donkey that they had chosen to buy someday.

"But come and see Gian-Carlo for yourself." Dino raised his basket to his shoulder and led the way. They visited the little donkey drowsing under the olive trees and admired his soft fur and sad, sweet eyes with their long lashes. Then the stranger said, "Now I should like to see some more of your father's pottery. Some that is not broken, if you please."

So Dino led him to the workshop.

The grandfather was making pots. He was turning moist clay on the wheel. He took a lump of it and set it on the wheel that was like a round table top that turned. As the clay whirled, he shaped it. Almost like magic it rose, took shape, and became a vase. Dino always thought this was the way a bud must open into a flower if you could see it happening before your eyes.

Then he showed the visitor the oven where the pots were baked until they were strong and dry. He showed the finished pots waiting to be painted and others, already painted, waiting to be sold. And the stranger liked the pots as much as Dino did.

He was in this part of Italy, he told them, to buy wares for his big shop in the north. He would like to order some of their pottery—some of these dishes and some of those. In fact, he kept on ordering so many that the grandfather began to laugh. He said that his head was turning faster than his wheel ever had.

After the stranger had gone, Dino and the grandfather began to count the money he had paid them. First Dino counted out enough to buy one of Gian-Carlo's soft gray legs. He piled the bills on the potter's wheel. He made a second pile as high, a third, and a fourth.

"Grandfather, just see!" he shouted "Just see, here's enough for the four legs, all of them."

And still he kept on counting. There were eight piles of bills when he had finished.

The old grandfather and Dino hugged each other so hard that the old man's knitted cap popped off his bald head. Then Dino jigged on the earthen floor until his bare blue feet began to feel warm.

When Papa came, tired and sad, up the steep winding way
with his unsold pots, Dino ran to meet him.

"A man came. I took him to see the church, even though I
was afraid of Old Agata. I showed him your pots and he thought
they were so beautiful that he bought many. And we've got
money at last to buy not four but eight of Gian-Carlo's legs, if
he had that many!" he told Papa. Then he added in a low voice,
"But I did break the best pots in my basket before that."

That night at the midnight service so far below in the town, Dino marched in the procession beside Mario. He carried a candle and on his feet were shoes of leather that made as good a sound as his friend's.

At the end of the service at midnight, when the bells in the tower were ringing and cannon crackers were bursting into thunder through the streets and echoing back from the mountain, Dino ran out into the square with a rocket. The stranger from the North had given it to him.

"Now that your family has money and perhaps can buy a donkey, you won't need to make one of his legs your choice for a present. Instead, please take this money and buy the very biggest rocket in the town. Call that your Birthday choice."

So now Dino's rocket screamed up into the air with a tail of sparks. It arched and swooped down like a firebird.

Dino hoped that the grandfather who was waiting at home because his legs were too old to come to town, had seen it. He would always remember how beautiful the rocket was, long after the stick lay cold upon the mountain.